First Facts™

Holidays and Culture

# Valentine's Day

## *A Day of Friendship and Love*

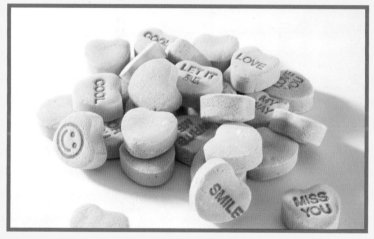

by Terri Sievert

**Consultant:**
David G. Hunter
Professor of Religious Studies
Iowa State University
Ames, Iowa

Capstone
*press*
Mankato, Minnesota

First Facts is published by Capstone Press,
151 Good Counsel Drive, P.O. Box 669, Mankato, Minnesota 56002.
www.capstonepress.com

*Library of Congress Cataloging-in-Publication Data*
Sievert, Terri.
    Valentine's Day : a day of friendship and love / by Terri Sievert.
    p. cm.—(First facts. Holidays and culture)
    Summary: "A brief description of what Valentine's Day is, how it started, and ways people
celebrate this cultural holiday"—Provided by publisher.
    Includes bibliographical references and index.
    ISBN-13: 978-0-7368-5393-4 (hardcover)
    ISBN-10: 0-7368-5393-6 (hardcover)
    1. Valentine's Day—Juvenile literature. I. Title. II. Series.
GT4925.S52 2006
394.2618—dc22                      2005015591

**Editorial Credits**
Jennifer Besel, editor; Juliette Peters, designer; Wanda Winch, photo researcher; Scott Thoms,
    photo editor

**Photo Credits**
Capstone Press/Gary Sundermeyer, 7; Karon Dubke, cover, 1, 21
Corbis/Fine Art Photographic Library, 12; PoodlesRock, 15; Sygma/Nogues, 19
Image courtesy of the Basilica di San Valentino, Terni, Italy, 11
Photo courtesy of the Starlight Cove Elementary School, Lantana, Florida, 20
Photodisc/Janis Christie, 16
PhotoEdit Inc./Michael Newman, 13; Myrleen Ferguson Cate, 14; Will Hart, 4–5
Stock Montage, Inc., 8

# Table of Contents

# Celebrating Valentine's Day

Red hearts dangle from a classroom ceiling. Kids zip around the room, delivering cards and treats. They smile and say, "Happy Valentine's Day!"

All around the world, children and adults get cards and candy. Valentine's Day is a time for people to show others they care.

# What Is Valentine's Day?

On the calendar, Valentine's Day is February 14. **Cultures** around the world celebrate this holiday in different ways. But all Valentine's Day **customs** honor friendship and love.

Valentine's Day was created as a **Christian** holiday. Today, the holiday is most often celebrated in places where many Christians live.

**Fact!**

Sending pressed white flowers, called snowdrops, to friends is a popular Valentine's Day custom in Denmark.

# A Roman Festival

No one really knows how Valentine's Day began. Some believe it started as an ancient **Roman** festival held on February 15. Romans believed the festival's customs helped women have children.

Over time, the focus of the holiday changed. This new celebration honored the legend of Saint Valentine.

**Fact!**

People once believed that birds chose mates on February 14. Some people think this is how Valentine's Day began.

# Legend of Saint Valentine

Valentine lived in Rome around the year 270. At that time, there was a law that made marriage illegal. A **legend** says Valentine performed secret marriages. When Rome's ruler found out, he had Valentine killed. About 200 years later, the pope made February 14 a day to remember Saint Valentine.

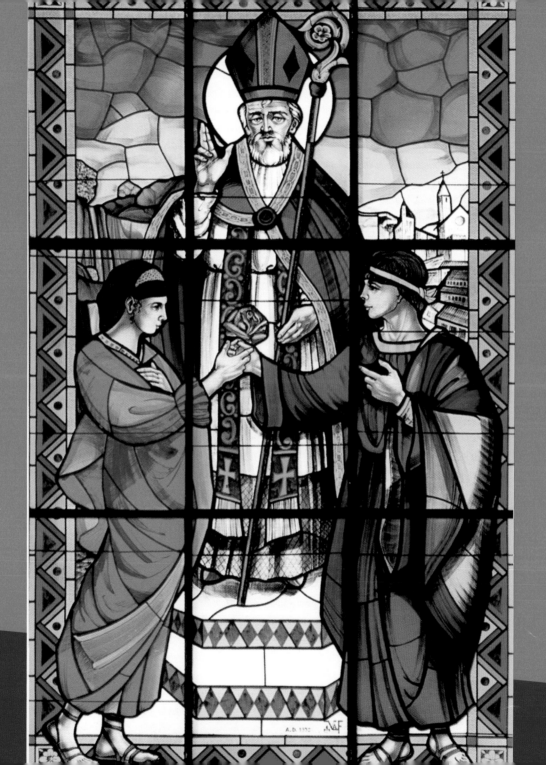

# A Day for Everyone

Valentine's Day used to be only a time for love. According to an English custom in the 1800s, the first man a woman saw that day would be the man she would one day marry.

Today, Valentine's Day cards and gifts are given to show friendship too. Everyone can celebrate this holiday by showing others they care.

# Red Hearts and Cupid

The heart is often thought to be where love comes from. So on Valentine's Day, red hearts are used as a **symbol** of love. Red hearts decorate windows, cards, and even clothing.

Long ago, Romans believed the god
**Cupid** shot arrows at people to make
them fall in love. Today, Cupid is another
popular Valentine's Day symbol.

# Flowers and Candy

Romans thought the red rose was the favorite flower of Venus, the goddess of love. Today, roses are a popular Valentine's Day gift.

"Sweets for my sweet" is a familiar saying on Valentine's Day. People give candy to their sweethearts. Chocolate in a heart-shaped box is a tasty present.

**Fact!**

Factories make billions of candy hearts each year for Valentine's Day. These treats have been made since 1900.

# Around the World

Valentine's Day is celebrated differently from country to country. In France, couples gather at "The Wall of I Love Yous." In Japan, women give men *honmei*, or true feeling, chocolates. Funny notes sent to friends, called *gaekkebrev,* are popular in Denmark.

Each culture has its own customs, but they all honor friendship and love. That's what makes Valentine's Day such a special time all around the world.

19

# Amazing Holiday Story!

In 2005, soldiers were fighting in Operation Iraqi Freedom. Students in Lantana, Florida, knew the soldiers missed their families. They decided to send valentine greetings to the soldiers.

On Valentine's Day, the students made a video. Everyone wore red, white, and blue. The students told the soldiers they cared about them. The video was a special way to wish the soldiers a happy Valentine's Day.

# Hands On: Puffy Valentine

You can make your own valentine for Valentine's Day. Give your valentine to someone you care about.

## What You Need

scissors
two sheets of construction paper
markers, stencils, or stickers
stapler
tissue paper

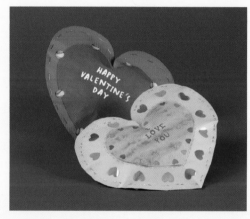

## What You Do

1. Cut two hearts of equal size out of the paper.
2. Use the markers, stencils, or stickers to decorate one side of each heart.
3. With the decorated sides facing out, staple the sides of the hearts together. Leave the top open.
4. Stuff the tissue paper inside the decoration to make it puff out.
5. Staple the tops of the hearts together to close your puffy valentine.

# Glossary

**Christian** (KRISS-chin)—a person who follows a religion based on the teachings of Jesus Christ

**culture** (KUHL-chur)—a people's way of life, ideas, art, customs, and traditions

**Cupid** (KYOO-pid)—the Roman god of love

**custom** (KUHSS-tuhm)—a tradition in a culture or society

**legend** (LEJ-uhnd)—a story handed down from earlier times; legends are often based on fact, but they are not entirely true.

**Roman** (ROH-muhn)—having to do with or coming from Rome; the people of ancient Rome are also called Romans.

**symbol** (SIM-buhl)—a design or an object that stands for something else

# Read More

**Haugen, Brenda.** *Valentine's Day.* Holidays and Celebrations. Minneapolis: Picture Window Books, 2004.

**Landau, Elaine.** *Valentine's Day: Candy, Love, and Hearts.* Finding Out About Holidays. Berkeley Heights, N.J.: Enslow, 2002.

**Rau, Dana Meachen.** *Valentine's Day.* A True Book. New York: Children's Press, 2001.

# Internet Sites

FactHound offers a safe, fun way to find Internet sites related to this book. All of the sites on FactHound have been researched by our staff.

**Here's how:**
1. Visit *www.facthound.com*
2. Type in this special code **0736853936** for age-appropriate sites. Or enter a search word related to this book for a more general search.
3. Click on the **Fetch It** button.

FactHound will fetch the best sites for you!

# Index